PSALMS FOR THE CHURCH CHOIR AND MUSIC GROUP

PSALMS FOR THE CHURCH CHOIR AND MUSIC GROUP

A COLLECTION OF ATTRACTIVE SETTINGS
COMPILED BY KEVIN MAYHEW

INDEXED FOR USE WITH THE THREE YEAR LECTIONARY

We hope you enjoy the music in this book. Further copies are available from your local music shop or Christian bookshop.

In case of difficulty, please contact the publisher direct by writing to:

The Sales Department
KEVIN MAYHEW LTD
Rattlesden
Bury St Edmunds
Suffolk
IP30 0SZ

Phone 01449 737978
Fax 01449 737834

Please ask for our complete catalogue of outstanding Church Music.

First published in Great Britain in 1997 by Kevin Mayhew Ltd.

© Copyright 1997 Kevin Mayhew Ltd.

ISBN 1 84003 001 1
ISMN M 57004 063 6
Catalogue No: 1450075

0 1 2 3 4 5 6 7 8 9

The texts and music in this book are protected by copyright and may not be reproduced in any way for sale or private use without the consent of the copyright owner.

Front cover: detail of an angel from *Christ in Glory*
by Domenico Chirlandaio (1449-1494).
Courtesy of Pinacoteca Volterra / SuperStock Ltd.
Reproduced by kind permission.
Cover design by Jaquetta Sergeant.

Music Editor: Alistair McPherson
Music setting by Daniel Kelly and Tracy Cracknell

Printed and bound in Great Britain

Contents listed by psalm number

Title		*Psalm*	*Page*
My God, why have you forsaken me?	Andrew Moore	21	8
God cares for all creation	Christopher Tambling	22	10
To you, O Lord, I lift up my soul	Andrew Moore	24	14
The Lord will bless his people with peace	Dom Alan Rees	28	16
Glorify the Lord	Peter Gonsalves	33	19
I will bless the Lord	Andrew Moore	33	20
Taste and see the goodness of the Lord	Andrew Moore	33	22
I'll turn my steps to the altar of God	Aniceto Nazareth	42	25
Behold, the Lamb of God	Gerard Markland	50	26
Hear my cry	Anthony D'Souza	60	28
For you my soul is thirsting	Andrew Moore	62	30
Faith in God	Aniceto Nazareth	70	32
With you, O God	Frances M. Kelly	72	34
On eagles' wings	Michael Joncas	90	36
Come, let us raise a joyful song	Mike Anderson	94	40
O that today you would listen to his voice	Andrew Moore	94	42
Blessed be God	Richard Lloyd	95	44
All the ends of the earth	Andrew Moore	97	46
Alleluia: all the earth	Andrew Moore	99	48
We are his people	Andrew Moore	99	50
Alleluia: praise God	Richard Lloyd	102 & 104	52
Send forth your Spirit, O Lord	Aniceto Nazareth	103	54
Give thanks to God	Christopher Tambling	117	56
O my Lord, within my heart	Estelle White	130	59
Yahweh, I know you are near	Dan Shutte	138	60
All the nations of the earth	Kevin Mayhew	148	62
Praise the Lord in his holy house	Frances M. Kelly	150	64

Contents listed alphabetically

Title		Psalm	Page
All the ends of the earth	Andrew Moore	97	46
All the nations of the earth	Kevin Mayhew	148	62
Alleluia: all the earth	Andrew Moore	99	48
Alleluia: praise God	Richard Lloyd	102 & 104	52
Behold, the Lamb of God	Gerard Markland	50	26
Blessed be God	Richard Lloyd	95	44
Come, let us raise a joyful song	Mike Anderson	94	40
Faith in God	Aniceto Nazareth	70	32
For you my soul is thirsting	Andrew Moore	62	30
Give thanks to God	Christopher Tambling	117	56
Glorify the Lord	Peter Gonsalves	33	19
God cares for all creation	Christopher Tambling	22	10
Hear my cry	Anthony D'Souza	60	28
I will bless the Lord	Andrew Moore	33	20
I'll turn my steps to the altar of God	Aniceto Nazareth	42	25
My God, why have you forsaken me?	Andrew Moore	21	8
O my Lord, within my heart	Estelle White	130	59
O that today you would listen to his voice	Andrew Moore	94	42
On eagles' wings	Michael Joncas	90	36
Praise the Lord in his holy house	Frances M. Kelly	150	64
Send forth your Spirit, O Lord	Aniceto Nazareth	103	54
Taste and see the goodness of the Lord	Andrew Moore	33	22
The Lord will bless his people with peace	Dom Alan Rees	28	16
To you, O Lord, I lift up my soul	Andrew Moore	24	14
We are his people	Andrew Moore	99	50
With you, O God	Frances M. Kelly	72	34
Yahweh, I know you are near	Dan Shutte	138	60

Foreword

This is not a definitive collection of psalms for the liturgical year. Rather, it is a gathering together of material that I know works well with choirs and congregations.

The result is a book that will provide a psalm (either the proper one assigned by the Lectionary or one of the seasonal alternatives) for most Sundays and Feasts. There is a comprehensive Index at the back of the book which will facilitate the choice of setting.

Psalms for the Church Choir and Music Group follows the spirit of The General Instruction of the Roman Missal which encourages communities to make choices dependant on their circumstances and abilities.

The settings are all for singing in unison, by either a cantor or choir, with organ accompaniment, though some have optional second parts or descants which may be taken by voice or instrument.

Where suitable there are guitar chords, but all the compositions may be accompanied by the sort of unspecified instrumental groups that come together for music making in church. The optional vocal descants and second parts, for example, can just as well be taken by a flute, violin or recorder. Lower parts, suitably transposed, will sound well on clarinet, while any bass instrument will simply work in with the left hand of the keyboard. Because every music group has a different instrumental line-up and musical ability, music directors will wish to make their own decisions about these matters.

The psalms in *Psalms for the Church Choir and Music Group* are tuneful, appealing and easily performed. That should be the spirit in which they are sung, imitating Jesus himself: 'After psalms had been sung they left for the Mount of Olives'.

Kevin Mayhew

PSALM 21
MY GOD, WHY HAVE YOU FORSAKEN ME?

Text: Susan Sayers
Music: Andrew Moore

© Copyright 1995 Kevin Mayhew Ltd.
It is illegal to photocopy music.

PSALM 22
GOD CARES FOR ALL CREATION

Text: Michael Forster
Music: Christopher Tambling

© Copyright 1996 Kevin Mayhew Ltd.
It is illegal to photocopy music.

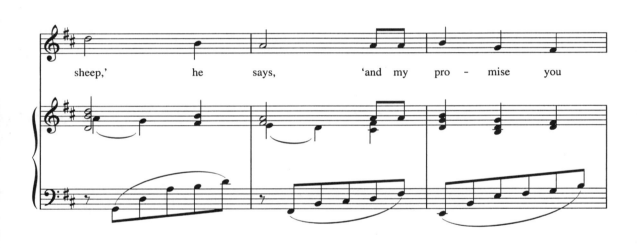

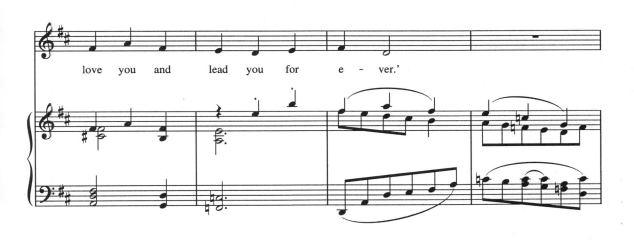
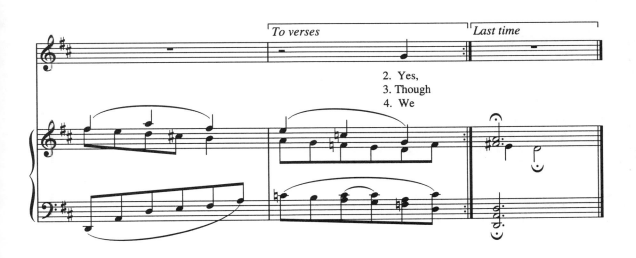

PSALM 24
TO YOU, O LORD, I LIFT UP MY SOUL

Text: Susan Sayers
Music: Andrew Moore

© Copyright 1996 Kevin Mayhew Ltd.
It is illegal to photocopy music.

PSALM 28

THE LORD WILL BLESS HIS PEOPLE WITH PEACE

Text: Susan Sayers
Music: Dom Alan Rees

© Copyright 1995 Kevin Mayhew Ltd.
It is illegal to photocopy music.

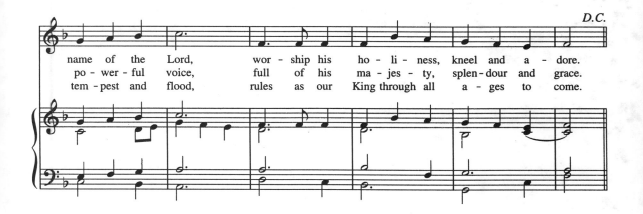

PSALM 33
GLORIFY THE LORD

Text and Music: Peter Gonsalves
Arranged by Christopher Tambling

© Copyright 1997 Kevin Mayhew Ltd.
It is illegal to photocopy music.

PSALM 33
I WILL BLESS THE LORD

Text: Susan Sayers
Music: Andrew Moore

© Copyright 1996 Kevin Mayhew Ltd.
It is illegal to photocopy music.

PSALM 33
TASTE AND SEE THE GOODNESS OF THE LORD

Text: Hubert J. Richards
Music: Andrew Moore

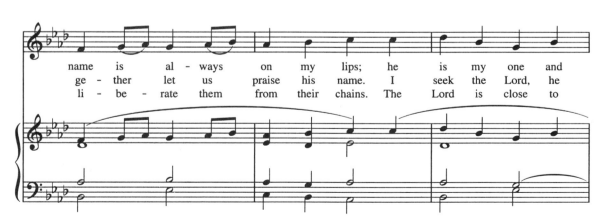

© Copyright 1996 Kevin Mayhew Ltd.
It is illegal to photocopy music.

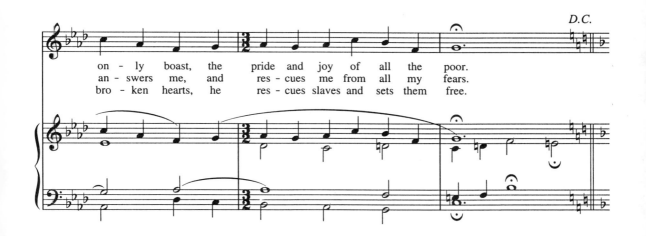

PSALM 42
I'LL TURN MY STEPS TO THE ALTAR OF GOD

Text and Music: Aniceto Nazareth
Arranged by Christopher Tambling

© Copyright 1984 Kevin Mayhew Ltd.
It is illegal to photocopy music.

PSALM 50
BEHOLD, THE LAMB OF GOD

Text: Damian Lundy
Music: Gerard Markland, arranged by Christopher Tambling

© Copyright 1997 Kevin Mayhew Ltd.
It is illegal to photocopy music.

PSALM 60
HEAR MY CRY

Text and Music: Anthony D'Souza
Arranged by Christopher Tambling

© Copyright 1997 Kevin Mayhew Ltd.
It is illegal to photocopy music.

PSALM 62
FOR YOU MY SOUL IS THIRSTING

Text: Susan Sayers
Music: Andrew Moore

PSALM 70
FAITH IN GOD

Text and Music: Aniceto Nazareth

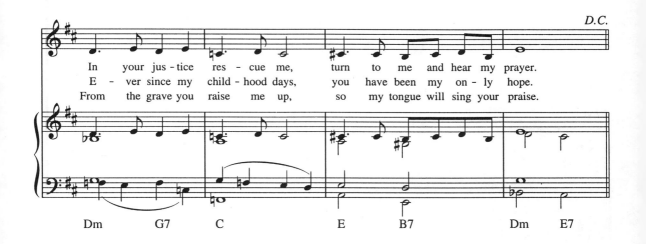

PSALM 72
WITH YOU, O GOD

Text: Frances M. Kelly
Music: Frances M. Kelly, arranged by Christopher Tambling

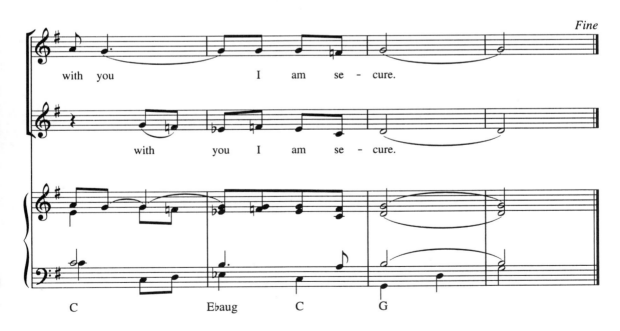

Words © Burns & Oates Ltd. Reprinted by permssion.
Music © Copyright 1984 Kevin Mayhew Ltd. All rights reserved.
It is illegal to photocopy music.

PSALM 90
ON EAGLES' WINGS

Text and Music: Michael Joncas
Arranged by Christopher Tambling

© Copyright 1979, 1991 New Dawn Music, 5536 NE Hassalo, Portland, OR 97213, USA.
All rights reserved. Used by permission.

PSALM 94
COME, LET US RAISE A JOYFUL SONG

Text and Music: Mike Anderson
Arranged by Adrian Vernon Fish

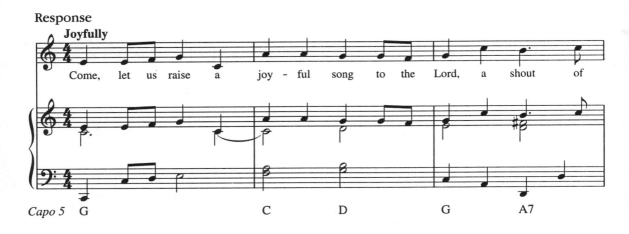

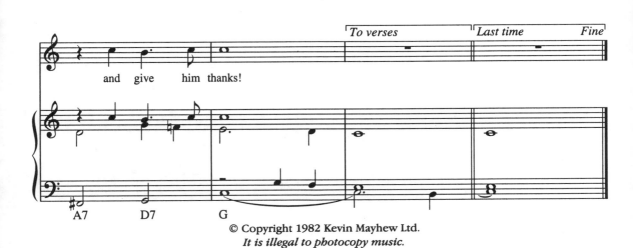

© Copyright 1982 Kevin Mayhew Ltd.
It is illegal to photocopy music.

PSALM 94
O THAT TODAY YOU WOULD LISTEN TO HIS VOICE

Text: Susan Sayers
Music: Andrew Moore

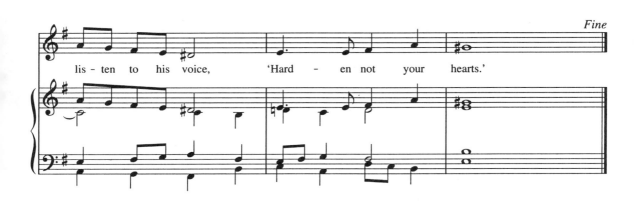

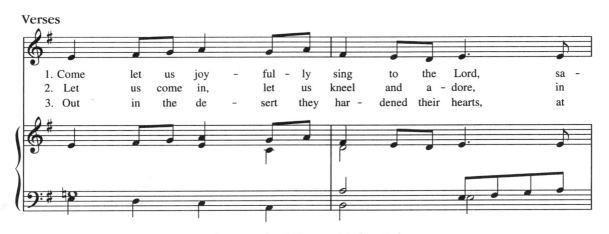

© Copyright 1995 Kevin Mayhew Ltd.
It is illegal to photocopy music.

PSALM 97
ALL THE ENDS OF THE EARTH

Text: Susan Sayers
Music: Andrew Moore

© Copyright 1995 Kevin Mayhew Ltd.
It is illegal to photocopy music.

PSALM 99
WE ARE HIS PEOPLE

Text: Susan Sayers
Music: Andrew Moore

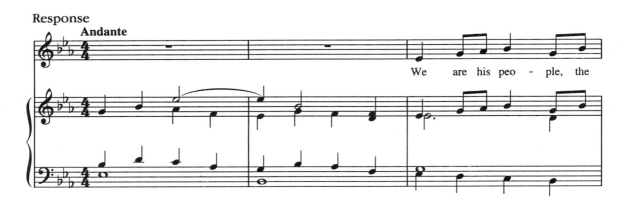

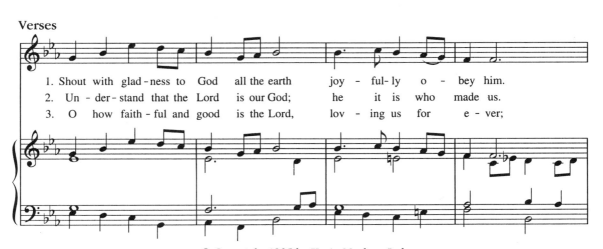

© Copyright 1995 by Kevin Mayhew Ltd.
It is illegal to photocopy music.

PSALMS 102 and 104
ALLELUIA: PRAISE GOD

Text: Hubert J. Richards
Music: Richard Lloyd

© Copyright 1995 Kevin Mayhew Ltd.
It is illegal to photocopy music.

PSALM 103
SEND FORTH YOUR SPIRIT, O LORD

Text and Music: Aniceto Nazareth

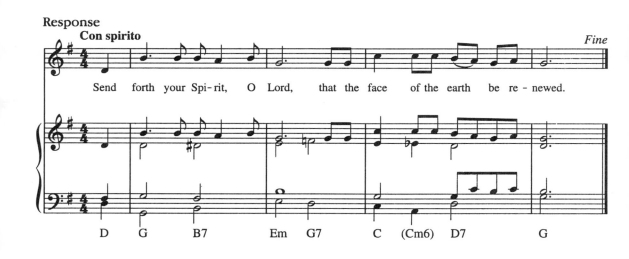

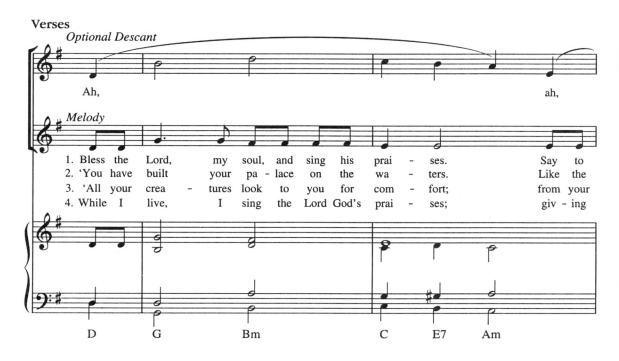

© Copyright 1996 Kevin Mayhew Ltd.
It is illegal to photocopy music.

Verses

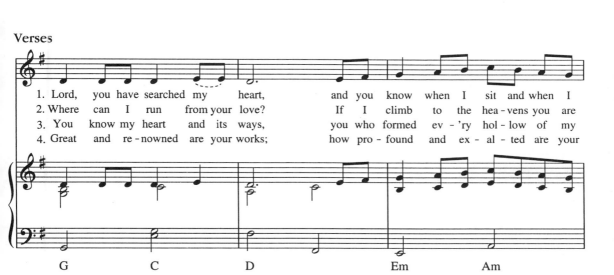

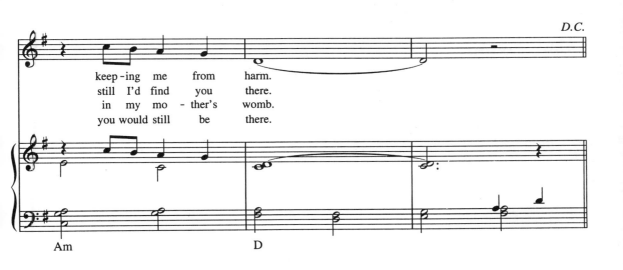

PSALM 148
ALL THE NATIONS OF THE EARTH

Text: Michael Cockett
Music: Kevin Mayhew, arranged by Adrian Vernon Fish

© Copyright McCrimmon Publishers, 10-12 High Street, Great Wakering,
Essex SS3 0EX. All rights reserved.
Reproduced by arrangement.

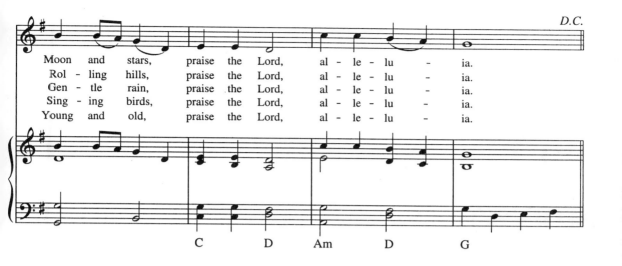

PSALM 150
PRAISE THE LORD IN HIS HOLY HOUSE

Text and Music: Frances M. Kelly
Arranged by Christopher Tambling

© Copyright 1997 Kevin Mayhew Ltd.
It is illegal to photocopy music.

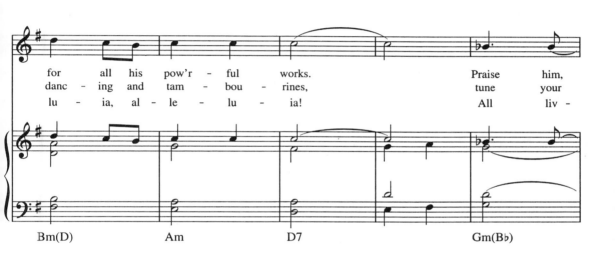

Index of Sunday and Feastday Psalms

Index of Sunday and Feastday Psalms

An asterisk indicates that the psalm listed is one of the seasonal psalms given in the Lectionary. All other texts are the proper psalm of the day.

	Psalm	Page
YEAR A		
THE SEASON OF ADVENT		
*To you, O Lord, I lift up my soul	24	14
CHRISTMAS DAY: MASS AT MIDNIGHT		
Blessed be God	95	44
THE SEASON OF CHRISTMAS: ALL OTHER MASSES		
*All the ends of the earth	97	46
THE BAPTISM OF THE LORD		
The Lord will bless his people with peace	28	16
ASH WEDNESDAY		
Behold, the Lamb of God	50	26
1ST SUNDAY OF LENT		
Behold, the Lamb of God	50	26
2ND SUNDAY OF LENT		
*On eagles' wings	90	36
3RD SUNDAY OF LENT		
O that today you would listen to his voice	94	42
4TH SUNDAY OF LENT		
God cares for all creation	22	10
5TH SUNDAY OF LENT		
*Behold, the Lamb of God	50	26
PASSION SUNDAY		
My God, why have you forsaken me?	21	8
HOLY THURSDAY		
*My God, why have you forsaken me?	21	8
GOOD FRIDAY		
*My God, why have you forsaken me?	21	8
EASTER VIGIL		
Send forth your Spirit, O Lord	103	54
Behold, the Lamb of God	50	26
Give thanks to God	117	56
EASTER SUNDAY		
Give thanks to God	117	56
4TH SUNDAY OF EASTER		
God cares for all creation	22	10
THE SEASON OF EASTER: ALL OTHER SUNDAYS		
*Give thanks to God	117	56
PENTECOST SUNDAY		
Send forth your Spirit, O Lord	103	54
THE MOST HOLY TRINITY		
*Come, let us raise a joyful song	94	40
2ND SUNDAY IN ORDINARY TIME		
*Taste and see the goodness of the Lord	33	22
3RD SUNDAY IN ORDINARY TIME		
*For you my soul is thirsting	62	30
4TH SUNDAY IN ORDINARY TIME		
*I will bless the Lord	33	20
5TH SUNDAY IN ORDINARY TIME		
*O that today you would listen to his voice	94	42
6TH SUNDAY IN ORDINARY TIME		
*O that today you would listen to his voice	94	42
7TH SUNDAY IN ORDINARY TIME		
Alleluia! Praise God	102 & 104	52
8TH SUNDAY IN ORDINARY TIME		
*I will bless the Lord	33	20
9TH SUNDAY IN ORDINARY TIME		
*I will bless the Lord	33	20
10TH SUNDAY IN ORDINARY TIME		
*Alleluia: all the earth	99	48
*We are his people	99	50
11TH SUNDAY IN ORDINARY TIME		
Alleluia: all the earth	99	48
We are his people	99	50
12TH SUNDAY IN ORDINARY TIME		
*For you my soul is thirsting	62	30
13TH SUNDAY IN ORDINARY TIME		
*I will bless the Lord	33	20
14TH SUNDAY IN ORDINARY TIME		
*I will bless the Lord	33	20

	Psalm	Page
15TH SUNDAY IN ORDINARY TIME		
*Come, let us raise a joyful song	94	40
16TH SUNDAY IN ORDINARY TIME		
*Alleluia: praise God	102 & 104	52
17TH SUNDAY IN ORDINARY TIME		
*O that today you would listen to his voice	94	42
18TH SUNDAY IN ORDINARY TIME		
*Come, let us raise a joyful song	94	40
19TH SUNDAY IN ORDINARY TIME		
*Alleluia: praise God	102 & 104	52
20TH SUNDAY IN ORDINARY TIME		
*Glorify the Lord	33	19
*I will bless the Lord	33	20
21ST SUNDAY IN ORDINARY TIME		
*I will bless the Lord	33	20
22ND SUNDAY IN ORDINARY TIME		
For you my soul is thirsting	62	30
23RD SUNDAY IN ORDINARY TIME		
Come, let us raise a joyful song	94	40
O that today you would listen to his voice	94	42
24TH SUNDAY IN ORDINARY TIME		
Alleluia: praise God	102 & 104	52
25TH SUNDAY IN ORDINARY TIME		
*I will bless the Lord	33	20
26TH SUNDAY IN ORDINARY TIME		
To you, O Lord, I lift up my soul	24	14
27TH SUNDAY IN ORDINARY TIME		
*For you my soul is thirsting	62	30
28TH SUNDAY IN ORDINARY TIME		
God cares for all creation	22	10
29TH SUNDAY IN ORDINARY TIME		
Blessed be God	95	44
30TH SUNDAY IN ORDINARY TIME		
*For you my soul is thirsting	62	30
31ST SUNDAY IN ORDINARY TIME		
O my Lord, within my heart	130	59
32ND SUNDAY IN ORDINARY TIME		
For you my soul is thirsting	62	30
33RD SUNDAY IN ORDINARY TIME		
*O that today you would listen to his voice	94	42
LAST SUNDAY IN ORDINARY TIME: OUR LORD JESUS CHRIST, UNIVERSAL KING		
God cares for all creation	22	10

YEAR B

	Psalm	Page
THE SEASON OF ADVENT		
*To you, O Lord, I lift up my soul	24	14
CHRISTMAS DAY: MASS AT MIDNIGHT		
Blessed be God	95	44
THE HOLY FAMILY		
Alleluia: praise God	102 & 104	52
THE SEASON OF CHRISTMAS: ALL OTHER MASSES		
*All the ends of the earth	97	46
ASH WEDNESDAY		
Behold, the Lamb of God	50	26
1ST SUNDAY OF LENT		
To you, O Lord, I lift up my soul	24	14
5TH SUNDAY OF LENT		
Behold, the Lamb of God	50	26
THE SEASON OF LENT: ALL OTHER SUNDAYS		
*Behold, the Lamb of God	50	26
*On eagles' wings	90	36
PASSION SUNDAY - EASTER SUNDAY See Year A		
6TH SUNDAY OF EASTER		
All the ends of the earth	97	46
7TH SUNDAY OF EASTER		
Alleluia: praise God	102 & 104	52
THE SEASON OF EASTER: ALL OTHER SUNDAYS		
Give thanks to God	117	56
PENTECOST SUNDAY		
Send forth your Spirit, O Lord	103	54
THE MOST HOLY TRINITY		
*We are his people	99	50
2ND SUNDAY IN ORDINARY TIME		
*I will bless the Lord	33	20
3RD SUNDAY IN ORDINARY TIME		
To you, O Lord, I lift up my soul	24	14
4TH SUNDAY IN ORDINARY TIME		
O that today you would listen to his voice	94	42
5TH SUNDAY IN ORDINARY TIME		
*I will bless the Lord	33	20
6TH SUNDAY IN ORDINARY TIME		
*Alleluia: praise God	102 & 104	52

	Psalm	Page
7TH SUNDAY IN ORDINARY TIME		
*Glorify the Lord	33	19
8TH SUNDAY IN ORDINARY TIME		
Alleluia: praise God	102 & 104	52
9TH SUNDAY IN ORDINARY TIME		
*O that today you would listen to his voice	94	42
10TH SUNDAY IN ORDINARY TIME		
*For you my soul is thirsting	62	30
11TH SUNDAY IN ORDINARY TIME		
*Alleluia: all the earth	99	48
12TH SUNDAY IN ORDINARY TIME		
*I will bless the Lord	33	20
13TH SUNDAY IN ORDINARY TIME		
*Glorify the Lord	33	19
14TH SUNDAY IN ORDINARY TIME		
*For you my soul is thirsting	62	30
15TH SUNDAY IN ORDINARY TIME		
*We are his people	99	50
16TH SUNDAY IN ORDINARY TIME		
God cares for all creation	22	10
17TH SUNDAY IN ORDINARY TIME		
*Come, let us raise a joyful song	94	40
18TH SUNDAY IN ORDINARY TIME		
*We are his people	99	50
19TH SUNDAY IN ORDINARY TIME		
Glorify the Lord	33	19
I will bless the Lord	33	20
Taste and see the goodness of the Lord	33	22
20TH SUNDAY IN ORDINARY TIME		
Glorify the Lord	33	19
I will bless the Lord	33	20
Taste and see the goodness of the Lord	33	22
21ST SUNDAY IN ORDINARY TIME		
Glorify the Lord	33	19
I will bless the Lord	33	20
Taste and see the goodness of the Lord	33	22
22ND SUNDAY IN ORDINARY TIME		
*O that today you would listen to his voice	94	42
23RD SUNDAY IN ORDINARY TIME		
*Glorify the Lord	33	19
24TH SUNDAY IN ORDINARY TIME		
*I will bless the Lord	33	20
25TH SUNDAY IN ORDINARY TIME		
*For you my soul is thirsting	62	30
26TH SUNDAY IN ORDINARY TIME		
*O that today you would listen to his voice	94	42
27TH SUNDAY IN ORDINARY TIME		
*Taste and see the goodness of the Lord	33	22
28TH SUNDAY IN ORDINARY TIME		
*For you my soul is thirsting	62	30
29TH SUNDAY IN ORDINARY TIME		
*We are his people	99	50
30TH SUNDAY IN ORDINARY TIME		
*Alleluia: all the earth	99	48
31ST SUNDAY IN ORDINARY TIME		
*For you my soul is thirsting	62	30
32ND SUNDAY IN ORDINARY TIME		
*I will bless the Lord	33	20
33RD SUNDAY IN ORDINARY TIME		
*For you my soul is thirsting	62	30
LAST SUNDAY IN ORDINARY TIME: OUR LORD JESUS CHRIST, UNIVERSAL KING		
*Come, let us raise a joyful song	94	40

YEAR C

	Psalm	Page
THE SEASON OF ADVENT		
*To you, O Lord, I lift up my soul	24	14
CHRISTMAS DAY: MASS AT MIDNIGHT		
Blessed be God	95	44
THE SEASON OF CHRISTMAS: ALL OTHER MASSES		
*All the ends of the earth	97	46
THE BAPTISM OF THE LORD		
Send forth your Spirit, O Lord	103	54
ASH WEDNESDAY		
Behold, the Lamb of God	50	26
1ST SUNDAY OF LENT		
On eagles' wings	90	36
3RD SUNDAY OF LENT		
Alleluia: praise God	102 & 104	52
4TH SUNDAY OF LENT		
Taste and see the goodness of the Lord	33	22

	Psalm	Page
THE SEASON OF LENT: ALL OTHER SUNDAYS		
*Behold, the Lamb of God	50	26
*On eagles' wings	90	36
PASSION SUNDAY - EASTER SUNDAY See Year A		
2ND SUNDAY OF EASTER		
Give thanks to God	117	56
4TH SUNDAY OF EASTER		
We are his people	99	50
THE SEASON OF EASTER: ALL OTHER SUNDAYS		
*Give thanks to God	117	56
PENTECOST SUNDAY		
Send forth your Spirit, O Lord	103	54
THE MOST HOLY TRINITY		
*Come, let us raise a joyful song	94	40
2ND SUNDAY IN ORDINARY TIME		
Blessed be God	95	44
3RD SUNDAY IN ORDINARY TIME		
*We are his people	99	50
4TH SUNDAY IN ORDINARY TIME		
Faith in God	70	32
5TH SUNDAY IN ORDINARY TIME		
*I will bless the Lord	33	20
6TH SUNDAY IN ORDINARY TIME		
*O that today you would listen to his voice	94	42
7TH SUNDAY IN ORDINARY TIME		
Alleluia: praise God	102 & 104	52
8TH SUNDAY IN ORDINARY TIME		
*Glorify the Lord	33	19
9TH SUNDAY IN ORDINARY TIME		
*Alleluia: all the earth	99	48
10TH SUNDAY IN ORDINARY TIME		
*Taste and see the goodness of the Lord	33	22
11TH SUNDAY IN ORDINARY TIME		
*Alleluia: praise God	102 & 104	52
12TH SUNDAY IN ORDINARY TIME		
For you my soul is thirsting	62	30
13TH SUNDAY IN ORDINARY TIME		
*For you my soul is thirsting	62	30
14TH SUNDAY IN ORDINARY TIME		
*We are his people	99	50
15TH SUNDAY IN ORDINARY TIME		
*Taste and see the goodness of the Lord	33	22
16TH SUNDAY IN ORDINARY TIME		
*Glorify the Lord	33	19
17TH SUNDAY IN ORDINARY TIME		
*I will bless the Lord	33	20
18TH SUNDAY IN ORDINARY TIME		
*For you my soul is thirsting	62	30
19TH SUNDAY IN ORDINARY TIME		
*We are his people	99	50
20TH SUNDAY IN ORDINARY TIME		
*Taste and see the goodness of the Lord	33	22
21ST SUNDAY IN ORDINARY TIME		
*Alleluia: all the earth	99	48
22ND SUNDAY IN ORDINARY TIME		
*O that today you would listen to his voice	94	42
23RD SUNDAY IN ORDINARY TIME		
*For you my soul is thirsting	62	30
24TH SUNDAY IN ORDINARY TIME		
Behold, the Lamb of God	50	26
25TH SUNDAY IN ORDINARY TIME		
*Glorify the Lord	33	19
26TH SUNDAY IN ORDINARY TIME		
*Taste and see the goodness of the Lord	33	22
27TH SUNDAY IN ORDINARY TIME		
O that today you would listen to his voice	94	42
28TH SUNDAY IN ORDINARY TIME		
All the ends of the earth	97	46
29TH SUNDAY IN ORDINARY TIME		
*We are his people	99	50
30TH SUNDAY IN ORDINARY TIME		
I will bless the Lord	33	20
31ST SUNDAY IN ORDINARY TIME		
*Alleluia: all the earth	99	48
32ND SUNDAY IN ORDINARY TIME		
*For you my soul is thirsting	62	30
33RD SUNDAY IN ORDINARY TIME		
All the ends of the earth	97	46
LAST SUNDAY IN ORDINARY TIME: OUR LORD JESUS CHRIST, UNIVERSAL KING		
*Taste and see the goodness of the Lord	33	22